To:

From:

Date:

You Are Essential

100 Inspirational Reminders of How Much You Matter

THOMAS NELSON
Since 1798

Published in Nashville, Tennessee, by Thomas Nelson. Thomas Nelson is a registered trademark of HarperCollins Christian Publishing, Inc.

Thomas Nelson titles may be purchased in bulk for educational, business, fundraising, or sales promotional use. For information, please email SpecialMarkets@ ThomasNelson.com.

Unless otherwise noted, Scripture quotations are taken from the Holy Bible, New International Version®, NIV®. Copyright © 1973, 1978, 1984, 2011 by Biblica, Inc. ® Used by permission of Zondervan. All rights reserved worldwide. www.zondervan. com. The "NIV" and "New International Version" are trademarks registered in the United States Patent and Trademark Office by Biblica, Inc. ®

Scripture quotations marked ESV are taken from the ESV® Bible (The Holy Bible, English Standard Version®). Copyright © 2001 by Crossway, a publishing ministry of Good News Publishers. Used by permission. All rights reserved.

Any internet addresses, phone numbers, or company or product information printed in this book are offered as a resource and are not intended in any way to be or to imply an endorsement by Thomas Nelson, nor does Thomas Nelson vouch for the existence, content, or services of these sites, phone numbers, companies, or products beyond the life of this book.

Library of Congress Cataloging-in-Publication Data

ISBN 978-1-4002-2844-7
ISBN 978-1-4002-2847-8 (eBook)
ISBN 978-1-4002-2846-1 (audio)

Printed in India

21 22 23 24 25 BRI 5 4 3 2 1

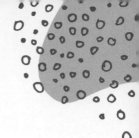

Introduction

You are essential. Yes, you!

You touch the lives of others every day with your words, your actions, and your choices, and you make a difference in those lives. Our world is better because of the kindness you speak with, the compassion you give out so freely, and the love you show to everyone around you. We all need one another, and you do so much to help and encourage both strangers and your loved ones alike.

There may be days when it feels like the work you do goes unnoticed or underappreciated, but it always matters. Your helping heart and dedication make the lives of so many significantly better.

For all the late nights, thankless tasks, and secret sacrifices, thank you. So many are very grateful for you, and you will always be essential.

1

Everyone Is Essential

Soft peace she brings; wherever she arrives
She builds our quiet as she forms our lives;
Lays the rough paths of peevish Nature even,
and opens in each heart a little heaven.

MATTHEW PRIOR

Most lives aren't lived in the spotlight, accomplishing big, news-worthy things. No, most of us live quiet lives.

We care for our families, serve in our communities, and work diligently at our jobs. Sometimes we assume that our quiet lives matter less than the big history-changing ones. But your life makes a bigger difference than you realize.

World leaders make policies and laws that affect each of us, but, so often, we feel those things indirectly. The truth is that the work that you do serving your family, friends, and community makes an impact that those people feel directly. Your words and actions matter to the happiness and comfort of the people you see each and every day. And that is essential.

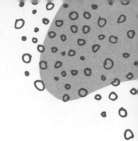

2

Look for Helpers

My mother would say to me, "Look for the helpers.
You will always find people who are helping."

FRED ROGERS

During the COVID-19 pandemic, so many essential workers stepped up to keep us all safe. They continued to go to work each day, risking their own health and the health of their families.

Dr. Kashif Chaudhry, a cardiac surgeon, and Dr. Naila Shereen, a chief resident, met and fell in love on medical mission trips to developing countries[1]. They were eager to put an end to their long-distance relationship and had a big overseas wedding and a luxurious honeymoon.

When the pandemic hit, they immediately scrapped their plans. They tied the knot in a small, socially distanced ceremony, and twelve hours later they were both back at work at their respective hospitals. It must have taken so much strength to leave each other, knowing that there was a very real risk one or both of them could get sick and die before they had the chance to really start their lives as husband and wife. Aren't you thankful for helpers like that?

Live your life
while you have
it. Life is a
splendid gift.
There is nothing
small in it.

FLORENCE NIGHTINGALE

3

Your Purpose Matters

Each day that we wake up and get the chance to live and love is a gift. Each of us has only so many days, so it is important that we live them well. Living well means something a little different to everyone, but most of us would agree that a life well lived includes love, kindness, and purpose.

Some people have a purpose that affects thousands, and others feel called to quieter projects that influence fewer people. But just because your purpose isn't flashy doesn't mean it's any less essential. On the contrary, the diligent work of people doing what they have been called to do keeps our world moving forward.

Whether your purpose is big or small, go after it with everything you've got, because what you are doing is essential to someone.

An early-
morning
walk is a
blessing for
the whole day.

HENRY DAVID THOREAU

4

Start the Day Right

The way we start our day matters. Rolling out of bed after hitting snooze three times, rushing to get dressed, and hurrying everyone out the door isn't anyone's idea of a good start. Beginning the day already behind, grumpy, and rushed rarely leads to a calm, productive morning of good work. In fact, you'll more likely be short-tempered, stressed, and not at your best.

Luckily, there is another way. By starting each day mindfully, you can feel kinder, more patient, and more joyful. When you are able to wake up earlier, you will have time to greet the day and mentally prepare for what's to come. Being able to take a few moments for prayer, a walk in the early morning air, or some gentle stretching will put you in a kind and patient frame of mind that is much easier to hold on to.

5

Treasure the Small Moments

Enjoy the little things, for one day you may look
back and realize they were the big things.

ROBERT BRAULT

An afternoon spent doing a puzzle with your little one or washing the car with your teenager doesn't exactly sound life-changing, does it? Especially when you have a full to-do list awaiting your attention.

But those small, quiet moments of quality time, laughter, or heart-to-heart conversation with the ones you love are what you'll still remember years from now. You won't remember the loads of laundry you should have done or the meal plan you needed to make. You'll remember the sweet giggles of delight as you put the final puzzle piece in place or the moment your normally tight-lipped kid opened up and asked for your advice.

Life sometimes throws obstacles in our path that interrupt our days. It can be frustrating. After all, we have places to go and things to do! But it's only when we slow down that we can spot the big things masquerading as little moments.

6

The Kindness of Strangers

The least of what you receive can be divided.
To help and share—that is the sum of all
knowledge, that is the meaning of art.

ELEONORA DUSÉ

Sometimes kindness is doing a good deed, but, more often, it's treating people like they matter. Every year, volunteer hairstylists, manicurists, and aestheticians come together at the Fred Jordan Mission of Los Angeles for the Mother's Make-Overs event[2] to pamper mothers who are experiencing homelessness or poverty. Each woman receives a manicure, haircut, and a lesson in applying makeup. They are sent home with goody bags filled with personal care products after a leisurely lunch.

Many of the women have never been to a salon or had a manicure. Being pampered and showered with attention can be emotional, and there are always women who leave the event crying happy tears. Of course, it's not just the haircut that means so much; it's being treated like they matter. It's that even in the midst of their struggles, they deserve to feel loved and beautiful.

Death leaves
a heartache no
one can heal;
love leaves a
memory no
one can steal.

7

You're Not Alone

Sometimes life hurts. You lose someone who you love. Money gets tight and you have to make difficult decisions. Unemployment looms. When you find yourself in free fall, grieving a loss that leaves you breathless, it can be difficult to imagine a day when you won't hurt so badly.

The good news is that none of us has to face grief alone. You are loved and there are people in your life who want to help you. It can be difficult to ask for help, to trust someone else with your vulnerability, but it is such a comfort when you do. Your friends and family can help lead you to healing, coax you forward when you aren't sure you can keep going, and provide a safety net that you can fall into if need be.

Of course, they aren't the only ones you can reach out to. God is with you and He will gladly help carry your burdens. His peace is always waiting for you.

Isn't it nice
to think that
tomorrow is a
new day with
no mistakes
in it yet?

L. M. MONTGOMERY

8

Give Yourself Grace

Some days it feels like nothing went your way. You had the worst luck—you ran late all day, your dog chewed up on your favorite shoes, you heard bad news, and your kid was sick. Or you just kept sticking your foot in your mouth—you messed up your presentation, accidentally offended a friend, and your boss caught you crying in the bathroom. *Yikes!* We've all had days like that.

Instead of lying awake, kicking yourself for everything that went wrong during your day, try forgiving yourself for your mistakes and giving yourself the grace not to have been your best self. If you can let those missteps go, they won't follow you into a new day. It can be difficult to do at first, but it will make such a difference in how you feel when you wake up to a fresh new morning.

9

You Can Be a Hero

For courage mounteth with occasion.

WILLIAM SHAKESPEARE

Most of us aren't trained experts in helping others, but we don't have to let that stop us from stepping up when we are needed.

Steve St. Bernard is an MTA bus driver who did exactly that.[3] One evening he found his seven-year-old autistic neighbor standing on her apartment's air conditioner on the third floor. He rushed over and stood beneath the air conditioner for seven excruciatingly long minutes. "I asked God . . . I said, 'Let me catch her, please. Don't let me miss,'" Steve told CNN. "I don't play baseball. I'm not a sportsman. I don't want to miss."

When the little girl jumped, Steve caught her, tearing a tendon in his shoulder in the process, but, despite the pain, he didn't let go. He could have sent the watching crowd to look for a professional or called for a fire truck to save her. He could have said, "Not me!" But he didn't. Instead, he saw someone in need and helped.

10

Love Knows No Boundaries

Therefore, as we have opportunity,
let us do good to all people.

GALATIANS 6:10

God explicitly instructs us to love one another. He doesn't say only to do good things for our friends or only love the people in our churches or only be kind to our family. No, He asks us to do good things and be a blessing to *everyone*. And that makes perfect sense because God loves every single one of us.

Thinking of strangers on the other side of the world (or even the other side of the country) as your neighbors can be difficult. You've never met them, you don't know their names, and you don't always understand why they do what they do. But in God's eyes, each person on this planet is your neighbor. Just as His love knows no boundaries, yours shouldn't either.

Today try to put yourself in a neighbor's shoes—someone very different from you—and ask yourself: *How can I love this person in a way that she wants to be loved?*

To love oneself is the beginning of a lifelong romance.

OSCAR WILDE

11

Love Yourself

Why does it always seem so much easier to be kind to others than to be truly kind to ourselves? We get so busy that we often forget to pencil self-care into our schedules, and our work suffers for it. We just can't effectively pour out of ourselves into those who need us if our own wells have run dry.

Self-care, despite what some might have you believe, isn't really bubble baths and face masks. It is the time and intentional care it takes to keep up your mental reserves of patience, peace, and generosity. When you stretch yourself too thin and forget to establish and enforce boundaries, those reserves will deplete fast.

We all want to do good in the world, but caring and kindness have to start with you. If you can be deliberate about caring for your mind, body, and soul, you will be so much better equipped to do good everywhere you go.

Blessed are
the hearts that
can bend; they
shall never
be broken.

FRANCIS DE SALES

12

Consider a New Viewpoint

We can all get a little set in our ways, and for good reason. Once we've made a decision or settled on a viewpoint, it becomes part of our identities, part of how we see ourselves. So if someone challenges that view, it can feel like a personal attack. That's when the walls go up, we get defensive, and double down on our opinion, no matter what anyone says.

The trouble is that it's next to impossible to know everything. We live in a world of information (and misinformation) overload. Even if we spent weeks researching a topic, we could never find every article and study out there, so there's just no way that every opinion we currently have is correct.

Once we accept that fact, it becomes easier to be open to new information and other viewpoints and to have empathy for people who believe differently. The next time someone challenges you, really listen to what he has to say. If we can focus more on understanding one another instead of on being right, we'll find that we all have more in common than it seems.

Do what you can, with what you have, where you are.

THEODORE ROOSEVELT

13

Make an Impact

The world is a mess, isn't it? So many people are out there hurting. It's enough to make you want to hide under the covers and never come out. It can feel impossible for one person to make any sort of difference in such a big world.

Luckily, it's not all up to you! No one person can fix the entire world. Let go of that expectation and start right where you are. Who do you know personally who could use a helping hand or a shoulder to cry on? Look for an issue in your neighborhood that needs a champion or a charity in your town that needs volunteers.

You don't have to find the perfect cause to take action. Every little bit of good you put out into the world will make a difference, and, eventually, you'll find a way and place to make an impact that's the perfect fit for you.

Act as if what
you do makes
a difference.
It does.

WILLIAM JAMES

14

Giving Is Contagious

Your choices matter. You might not see the effects they have, but that doesn't mean that they aren't there. When you choose to help someone else, to be kind and compassionate, it can have a big ripple effect.

When Anthony DeGuilio decided to donate his kidney to a stranger, he chose compassion.[4] He didn't know anyone personally who was sick, but he knew he could save a life, and so he did. He never could have guessed that he was setting off a chain reaction that would save four lives instead of just one.

Anthony's kidney went to Barbara Asofsky, whose husband decided to donate his kidney in turn. He was matched with Alina Binder, whose father was inspired to donate his kidney to Andrew Novak, whose sister then donated her kidney to Luther Johnson. Each transplant was performed on the same day.

None of the donors was a match for their own loved one, but after seeing Anthony's generous gift, they were inspired to do the same. Turns out, making a difference can be contagious.

Happiness is like a butterfly which, when pursued, is always beyond our grasp, but, if you will sit down quietly, may alight upon you.

15

Learn to Be Patient

It can be so tough to wait. Sometimes it's easier to hear that dreaded no than it is to wait, hanging out in that space between what we've got and what we want. Waiting makes us feel like we're not doing anything productive. People, by nature, are hardwired to keep moving forward, to adapt to new situations quickly so they don't get left behind. Having to wait stalls our momentum, and nobody likes that!

But waiting can be a blessing. When you are delayed, it forces you to stop and reexamine your motivations, your actions, and your goals. The possibility of a no means you have to think of a plan B. You can use the waiting time to prepare yourself for the very real possibility of a change of course, the end of a road, or a different destination altogether. Patience sees the opportunities hidden in the waiting and makes good use of them.

Any concern
too small to
be turned into
a prayer is too
small to be made
into a burden.

CORRIE TEN BOOM

16

Out of Our Control

Have you heard the expression, "Make a mountain out of a molehill"? It means to make a big deal out of something small. We're all guilty of that sometimes! How often have you been kept awake at night worrying over a necessary confrontation that turns out to be less confrontation and more lighthearted conversation?

We allow ourselves to be plagued with anxiety over the smallest things because we feel our circumstances are out of control. And they are. Even though it's tough to admit, no one has that much control over their lives. Any one of us could get sick, or be in an accident, or find ourselves in the midst of a natural disaster. We can't control the economy or politics or diseases. Obsessing and stressing may make us feel like we have control, but we don't. In fact, obsessing and stressing actually make us feel worse.

The only thing we have control over is how we react to any given situation. We can react by worrying or we can choose to trust God with our lives and circumstances, knowing that He is always in control.

A hero is someone
who has given
his or her life to
something bigger
than oneself.

JOSEPH CAMPBELL

17

Everyday Heroes

The word *hero* gets thrown around a lot. A friend who brings you coffee on a busy day might seem like a hero in that moment, but the real heroes are the ones who put themselves in danger for the good of others. We often think of police officers, members of the armed services, firefighters, and other first responders—and they are, undoubtedly, heroes.

However, there are other everyday people who become heroes in a crisis, risking their lives to help. Volunteers who clear rubble after earthquakes or paddle out into floodwaters to rescue survivors are heroes. So are the doctors and nurses on the front lines battling diseases.

The good, dependable folks who go to work even in the midst of terror attacks, pandemics, and natural disasters are pretty heroic too. They rarely get honors for their service, but without them we wouldn't be able to buy groceries, send our kids to school, have clean buses and bathrooms, buy gas, or any of the other countless things that keep our country running.

So thank an everyday hero today.

A friend is one
who overlooks
your broken fence
and admires
the flowers in
your garden.

18

Be Thankful for Friendship

Friendship is such a gift, and you are lucky indeed if you have a handful of close friends who know everything about you and love you just as you are. In a world where you always seem to need to be "on," never showing weakness or vulnerability, friendships like that are extra-important.

Isn't it nice to be able to pour yourself out to your friends, not needing to hide your insecurities or pretend to be anything but yourself? Doesn't it fill up your soul to talk and laugh and just *be* with the people who love you best?

Take a few minutes today to let your friends know how much they mean to you. Give them a call or write them a note to say thank you for all of the love and light they add to your life.

As night the life-inclining stars best shows, so lives obscure the starriest souls disclose.

GEORGE CHAPMAN

19

You're a Miracle

Go outside tonight and look up at the stars. Count as many of them as you can. The longer you look, the smaller you will feel.

Isn't it amazing that out of the vastness of space you are standing in this exact place at this exact time? The chances of your being born, just as you are, is more than one in four hundred trillion.[5] Crazy! It's truly a miracle that you are here.

So what are you, as a living, breathing miracle, going to do with your one miraculous life? You owe it to yourself to make it count. Take the time to find what you are passionate about. Dig deep and discover your purpose. Discover how you can use your unique strengths to make the difference in this world that you were born to make.

You have to do the right thing. It may not be in your power, may not be in your time, that there'll be any fruit. . . . You may never know what results come from your action. But if you do nothing, there will be no result.

MAHATMA GANDHI

20

Do the Right Thing

Doing good makes you feel good. Good deeds and kind words can have truly far-reaching effects, but most of us don't do good for the glory. We are kind because it's the right thing to do and treating others well makes us feel all warm and fuzzy inside.

Everyone gets discouraged sometimes, especially when they can't see any results from their hard work. It's special when you do get the chance to see how your actions make an impact. When that happens, celebrate it! Then tuck that memory away in your mind to bring out whenever you need a push to keep going.

Even if you never see the results of the good you are putting out into the world, just know that someone out there is benefiting from what you have done. Good leads to more good. Keep it up and trust that the results will come eventually!

"You are special, and so is your neighbor" — that part is essential: that you're not the only special person in the world. The person you happen to be with at the moment is loved, too.

FRED ROGERS

21

Love Everyone

Each of us matters to someone. Your mailman is a beloved husband. Your child's teacher is a cherished daughter. The barista at your favorite coffee shop is someone's best friend. Think about *your* people. How would you want them to be treated by strangers?

Each of us deserves love, kindness, and respect. Life is challenging. We can all fall into thinking that our people and our lives matter most sometimes. But the truth is that we all need each other. Every person you meet deserves to be treated like they are one of *your* people—the people you love and cherish most. If we can all remember to treat others with that kind of love, imagine what a difference it would make!

22

What Others Think Doesn't Matter

Start a huge, foolish project, like Noah. . . . It makes
absolutely no difference what people think of you.

RUMI

What others think about you is none of your business. Repeat
that to yourself as often as you need to. There will always be
people who judge you or disagree with your choices. You can't
control that. But you can control whether you let those people
stop you from creating the life you want.

A school plan that works well for other families may not
be the right fit for yours. That cushy job your coworkers all
want may sound like torture to you. That's okay. The charitable
organization that you've been dreaming of starting may not
make any sense to your friends. Don't let that stop you.

Each of us has unique gifts and a unique purpose that we
are here to fulfill. Your purpose might seem as huge and foolish
as Noah's ark was to outsiders, but Noah didn't give up when
he was ridiculed and neither should you.

23

An Attitude of Gratitude

From every place below the skies
The grateful song, the fervent prayer,—
The incense of the heart,—may rise
To heaven, and find acceptance there.

JOHN PIERPONT

Gratitude isn't just remembering to count your blessings. Gratitude is an attitude, a way of thinking about everything in your life that has the power to change your entire outlook. When we lean into the truth that each minute, hour, and day is a gift, we see the world around us with fresh eyes.

A grateful heart points us to ways we can help and honor others. It highlights places where we can do good. And it nudges us to speak up to make the world better for everyone, not just ourselves.

Cultivating an attitude of gratitude is something that pays off in spades. When you are grateful for everything you have and the opportunities in front of you, you will find that life feels lighter and you are more joyful. Life is sweeter when you see and appreciate all that it is.

Have a heart that never hardens, and a temper that never tires, and a touch that never hurts.

CHARLES DICKENS

24

Don't Have a Hard Heart

When life becomes difficult and exhausting, it would be so easy to allow yourself to become bitter, angry, or jaded. And, really, no one would blame you. The real challenge in life is not to let the world get you down. It takes true strength to remain open, curious, warm, empathetic, and vulnerable, but it's precisely those qualities that allow people to connect with one another.

A hard heart keeps love from getting in. A quick temper and an angry mind keep peace and joy at bay. A hurtful touch only adds trauma and damage to a world that already has too much of all that.

But a generous heart warms everyone around it. A slow temper and quick smile sow laughter and understanding. And a touch that heals leaves the world better than it was.

We must learn to reawaken and keep ourselves awake, not by mechanical aids, but by an infinite expectation of the dawn.

HENRY DAVID THOREAU

25

Stand Firm in the Storms

It's so tempting to give up on your dreams and plans when life throws you a curveball. After all, some days it's truly the best you can do to shower, go to work, and keep everyone fed. When the skies are all storm clouds and thunder, to keep dreaming can feel impossible, but don't give up. Hang on, even if it's just by a single thread.

When you are standing in the middle of a storm, you can't see beyond the rain right in front of you. The best thing you can do is put your head down and keep placing one foot in front of the other, following that single thread out of the dark night and into the bright morning. No storm lasts forever. It might take some time, but the sunshine will come. And when it does, you can start weaving that single thread from a dream into plans— and from plans into a new, shining reality.

Success in life is founded upon attention to the small things rather than to the large things; to the everyday things nearest to us rather than to the things that are remote and uncommon.

BOOKER T. WASHINGTON

26

Take Care of the Little Things

There is so much beauty in the everyday moments. Like the way the sunlight bathes the floor in a golden glow at sunset or how sweetly your little ones hug each other.

When we are able to slow down, even a little, it becomes easier to spot and be grateful for those moments of everyday beauty. Once we are noticing those little details of life, we are able to spot places that may need more nurturing from us. Like the washing machine that's acting funny and should be repaired before it breaks down. Or the kid who is a little afraid at bedtime and would feel braver with some extra attention.

The little things in life, both the beautiful and the messy, have the power to trip us up or to become the foundation for our success. So don't forget to take the time to pay attention before those little things turn into bigger things.

Don't just count your blessings. Be the blessing other people count on.

27

Be a Blessing

For the next week, instead of counting your blessings each night, try counting the times you were a blessing to someone else for that day. Not sure where to start? Here are a few ideas:

- Make dinner for your partner and do the dishes.
- Bake something yummy and drop it off at your local hospital, police station, or firehouse.
- Buy coffee for your coworker.
- Take on an unwanted task and handle it without complaining.
- Fill your car's cup holder with cash to give out to the needy.
- Mow the grass, rake leaves, or shovel snow for an elderly neighbor.
- Offer to babysit your sister's kids so she can have a few hours to herself.
- Host friends for brunch and tell them all how much they mean to you and why.

You'll find that blessing others will overflow you with gratitude. Don't wait. Start small, but start today.

I think I have learned that the best way to lift one's self up is to help someone else.

BOOKER T. WASHINGTON

28

Help Others in Need

When the COVID-19 lockdown came to England, one hotel stepped up to help people who had been forgotten. The upscale Fownes Hotel invited approximately fifty people experiencing homelessness to stay in their own rooms until restrictions ended.[6] Half of the hotel staff agreed to keep working to care for the unusual guests, providing fresh towels, linens, and three meals a day.

The hotel also worked with a local homeless charity to host workshops for their new guests on topics like overcoming addiction, finding government welfare benefits, and securing places to live after they left the hotel. The hotel's guests would have been at high risk for exposure to the virus had they remained on the streets. Because the hotel staff was willing to see the homeless population as hurting people in need instead of a nuisance, they likely saved many lives and gave hope to people who won't ever forget their generosity.

29
Go Outside

Live in the sunshine, swim the sea, drink the wild air.

RALPH WALDO EMERSON

When your days start feeling blah, it's a sure sign that it's time to shake things up and reconnect with the fierce beauty of nature. These days, most of our jobs keep us indoors. We sit under artificial light, breathe recycled air, and only catch the occasional glimpse of the sky. We just weren't made to live that way!

The next time you have a day off, get outside. Go for a hike through a lush forest, or climb up to the top of a cliff for a breathtaking view. Lie in the soft, green grass and look at the clouds dancing across the blue sky. Let the sun warm your face as you run through swirling leaves and a breeze tangles your hair. Dive into the ocean or a lake. Wade through a creek and float on the water, cold and smooth as silk against your skin.

Nature calls to us, beckoning us out into the fresh, sweet-smelling air. Go answer it.

30

It's Never Too Late

To my way of thinking it is not the years in your life but
the life in your years that counts in the long run.

If you had made it to age one hundred, you might be ready to
sit back and take it easy. Captain Sir Tom Moore of the UK
had a different idea.[7] When the coronavirus pandemic forced
England into lockdown, he started walking laps around his backyard to raise money in support of the UK's National Health
Service. Within a short amount of time, he had raised more
than thirty million pounds and walked one hundred laps.

It was quite a feat for the World War II veteran, who gets
around using a walker. His slow walks for charity inspired millions around the world, including the Queen of England herself.
She knighted Captain Tom at Windsor Castle as soon as the
lockdown was lifted.

Imagine the inspiring things you still have the opportunity
to do. It's never too late to get started!

The smallest
good deed is
better than the
grandest good
intention.

31

A Small Gesture

The little, everyday things are what make up a friendship. It's the text chains, the calls to check in, the drop-ins for a friendly chat or dinner, the prayers, the shoulder to cry on, the ear to listen, and the celebrations that weave together a friendship that stands the test of time.

Is there someone in your life whom you would like to become your friend? Maybe that cool mom at the playgroup or your new coworker with the great style? Start with something small and make the first move. Bring her a coffee or suggest lunch together. Ask her where she got her cute boots or what she's reading.

Chances are she could use a new friend too. All it takes is one little gesture to lead to another, and before you know it, she'll be dropping by for a chat and you'll be wondering what took you so long to reach out.

Keep good company,
read good books,
love good things,
and cultivate
soul and body
as faithfully
as you can.

LOUISA MAY ALCOTT

32

Read Good Books

The ideas and words that you fill your mind with become part of who you are eventually. If you watch nothing but reality TV and only read celebrity gossip magazines, will you be thinking about finding your purpose and making a difference in the world? Or, more likely, the latest fads and which B-list starlet is getting liposuction?

When you read books that challenge you and illustrate different perspectives, your empathy for others grows and you gain knowledge about other cultures and communities. When you prioritize time with friends who inspire and uplift you, you will inspire and uplift others. When you devote yourself to causes and issues that mean something special to you, you will make an impact that matters.

You only have one wild and wonderful life. You get to decide who you will be and how you will use it. Choose wisely.

A man who can laugh at himself is truly blessed, for he will never lack for amusement.

JAMES CARLOS BLAKE

33

Learn to Laugh at Yourself

We all make mistakes. We all fall flat on our faces, trip up, and embarrass ourselves. We all get overwhelmed and make a big deal out of something small. We all misunderstand sometimes. We can let these things lay us low and carry them around with us—covered in shame—or we can choose to give ourselves grace and learn from them.

When you can laugh at your mishaps and grow from what you've learned, you will find that you succeed more often than you fail. If each failure teaches you something, then you can use those lessons to overcome and do better until you reach your goals.

So embrace the mistakes. Don't take gaffes too seriously. Let yourself giggle through the embarrassment. And, if you mess up daily like so many of us do, take comfort in knowing that at least your life will always be full of laughter.

Those who cannot change their minds cannot change anything.

GEORGE BERNARD SHAW

34

Learn to Reconsider

It is perfectly acceptable to change your mind. None of us knows everything—how could we? We are always learning new things and finding new information. As we grow, our views and opinions will grow too. Holding tightly to convictions that we have outgrown doesn't serve us and, more often than not, holds us back.

Are there any beliefs you are holding onto because that's what you've always believed? When was the last time you challenged your thinking? Does that belief stand up to close scrutiny? Does learning about a new perspective give you pause? If it does, then it's a good indicator that you need to dig deeper and possibly rethink your stance.

There's no shame in learning and growing and changing what you believe and stand for. No one gains wisdom by refusing to consider anything new.

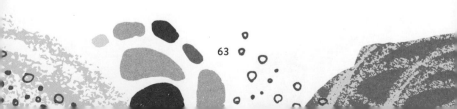

Piglet noticed that even though he had a Very Small Heart, it could hold a rather large amount of Gratitude.

A. A. MILNE

35

Choose to Be Grateful

Our hearts were built to be filled with love, joy, and gratitude. Today, make a list of all of the things that bring you joy and make your life more filled with love. These can be big things like a vacation to Italy or small things like leisurely drinking a hot cup of coffee every morning. Serious things like reading a new book or silly things like dancing in the kitchen when no one else is home. Or even romantic things like a date night with your sweetheart.

Once you have finished your list, tape it on your bathroom mirror or somewhere else you see often. Try to do as many of the things on your list as you can every day. There's no point in putting off for tomorrow the things that make us grateful for our lives. Choose joy for yourself today!

36

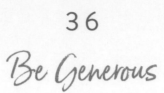

Be Generous

If you have much, give of your wealth; if
you have little, give of your heart.

ARAB PROVERB

Shetara Sims, a single mom in Kansas City, was down to her last seven dollars when she found a one-dollar bill and used it to buy a lottery ticket.[8] She won one hundred dollars. Instead of keeping the money, Shetara donated it to the family of a local police officer who had been wounded in the line of duty.

Shetara wanted to give back to the police department that had been there for her when her oldest daughter was killed in 2012. The officer on the phone urged her to keep the money, but Shetara was adamant that she wanted the police to know they were supported.

"To hear her call and just express thanks for no reason other than she's thankful, it's really impactful to us, and it's really touching to us," police Sgt. Jake Becchina said. Her generous donation such an impact in the police precinct, they wanted to help her too. The Kansas City police raised more than $145,000 to help this generous woman and her family.

37

Solve the Problem

Take time to deliberate, but when the time for
action has arrived, stop thinking and go in.

NAPOLÉON BONAPARTE

Is there something you see on the news that just breaks your
heart? An injustice that you long to make right? A group that
seems forgotten of which you want to remind others? A policy
or law that seems more hurtful than helpful? Don't you wonder
who is going to do something about these problems?

These things that break your heart and fill you with sorrow
aren't going to be solved until someone like you steps up to
solve them. When you get that sinking feeling in your heart
about something, it's usually a sign that fixing that problem may
be a part of your purpose. Each of us has the potential to make a
big impact on the world. The best way that you can do that is by
noticing when something seems wrong and being brave enough
to step up to help make it right.

We can't help
everyone, but
everyone can
help someone.

RONALD REAGAN

3 8

What Can You Knit?

When bushfires tore through the Australian outback in 2019, Australia's unique animals were threatened. Firefighters were able to rescue hundreds of koalas, but many of them suffered from smoke damage and burnt paws.[9] The little marsupials needed something to protect their healing paws.

Craft enthusiasts from all over the world responded to the call and knitted tiny koala mittens. Animal hospitals in Australia were soon inundated with packages of soft, adorable mittens. Once enough mittens had been sent in, people around the globe donated money to support the koalas' care, raising more than two million dollars in a matter of weeks.

You may not be able to devote all of your time to working for a charity, but there are people and animals that you can help. Sometimes all it takes is something as simple as knitting needles and a ball of yarn.

She was conscious that the things she did were the things she had always wanted to do.

ZELDA FITZGERALD

39

Find a Way to Help

No one else in the world is exactly like you. No one else has your particular combination of strengths, weaknesses, experiences, disappointments, loves, jobs, and a million other factors that make you *you*. You are special.

So doesn't it seem possible that there's an issue or problem out there in the world that needs your unique combination of qualifications to solve? It's unlikely that you are going to end world hunger all on your own, but so many smaller issues are in each city, town, community, and neighborhood. Maybe your problem to tackle is helping your child's school raise money for new textbooks. Or perhaps your issue is helping lonely seniors by leading an art class at your local retirement home.

The only way to find your cause is to get out there and try. Think about everything you bring to the table and look for someone who needs you.

40

What Is Forgiveness?

It is not what we take up, but what we
give up, that makes us rich.

HENRY WARD BEECHER

When someone hurts you, the pain can feel so incredibly heavy, especially if you were hurt by someone you loved and trusted. You may be able to push past it and keep going, but that heaviness will stay with you until you can find a way to forgive.

Forgiveness seems like it should be something you grant to someone who has wronged you, absolution that erases their actions. But that's not really it. Forgiveness is something you do for yourself as much as for the other person. It happens when you are able to work through the pain and lay down the weight of those hurts. You don't have to forget what happened or trust that person again, but forgiveness allows you to move forward—a little lighter and a little wiser.

41

Show Love to Everyone

"You shall treat the stranger who sojourns with you as the native among you, and you shall love him as yourself, for you were strangers in the land of Egypt: I am the LORD your God."

LEVITICUS 19:34 ESV

What would you be willing to do to give your family a better life? If you found yourself living under a corrupt government, in the middle of a war zone, or in an area devastated by natural disasters, would you stay and do your best to survive? Or seek a new land where your children had a better chance to grow up?

New families seek refuge in foreign lands every day, hoping to find peace and the chance to build a better life for themselves. God calls each of us to welcome the stranger with open arms, treating them with respect and kindness.

It's human nature to fall into an us versus them mentality when confronted with someone different. But if we can focus on seeing each person as a child of God, He will help us find a way forward to live together in harmony.

I'm not afraid
of storms, for
I'm learning
how to sail
my ship.

LOUISA MAY ALCOTT

42

Choose to Adjust Your Sails

We always have choices in life. Sometimes we might not like the choices in front of us, but we are always able to choose. We can't always control our circumstances and we certainly can't control the actions of others, but we can always control how we respond in each situation.

We can choose to see ourselves as victims and the world as uncaring. We can choose to act only in our own best interests. We can choose to hold onto anger and resentment. We can choose to give up. But does any of that sound like a life you would want for yourself?

Instead we can choose healing and forgiveness. We can choose positivity and hope and to keep going, even when it's tough. We can choose to create a life filled with love and laughter and joy even when it's full of challenges and sorrow.

If your life feels off course, adjust your sails and steer toward better choices.

Experience is the name so many people give to their mistakes.

OSCAR WILDE

43

Adversity Is a Great Teacher

Wouldn't it be nice if we could all become the best versions of ourselves by hanging out by the pool and sipping fruity drinks? Or snuggling up under a cozy blanket in front of the fire with a mug of hot cocoa? Sadly, coziness and comfort just don't go hand in hand with personal growth.

The times we grow the most are when we face adversity and feel decidedly uncomfortable. How we handle life's challenges teaches us lessons we need to learn. Think about the last challenge you faced and how you felt when you came out on the other side. Weren't you proud of yourself for being strong and figuring things out?

The next time you find yourself staring down something tough, remember that. Remind yourself that this isn't so much a challenge as it is an opportunity to learn and grow.

44

You Have Potential

What lies behind us and what lies before us are
tiny matters compared to what lies within us.

Each of us, regardless of where we come from, carries the potential to do great things inside of us. It doesn't matter if we were born with nothing, grew up with silver spoons in our mouths, or fall somewhere in between. Where we come from doesn't matter if we have the drive, ambition, and vision to make our dreams a reality.

Seeing someone with a wealth of resources succeeding easily in something that you struggle with can be disappointing. But don't let that stop you. Your ideas, your passion, and your perspective are different and essential to your vision. No one can take those away from you.

Keep your head down and keep chasing what you want. When you get there, your unique spirit will be enough to set you apart from the pack.

45

Spend Time with Loved Ones

You will never regret not having passed one more
test. . . . You will regret time not spent with a
husband, a friend, a child, or a parent.

BARBARA BUSH

Think about the people in your life who matter most to you.
When was the last time you gave them your complete, undi-
vided attention? Without sneaking peeks at your phone or
thinking about work instead of what they said? If it's been a
while, then today is the perfect day to give them your time.

Grab a board game and play with your kids. In between
turns, ask them about their worries, hopes, and dreams. Pick up
takeout, and surprise your sweetheart with a candlelit dinner.
Bring coffee to your parents, and pull out photo albums to rem-
inisce about old times. Take your dog for an extralong walk. Call
your best friend to catch up and make plans to see each other.

Those afternoons of connection will be something you will
remember for years to come.

Those blessings
are sweetest
that are won
with prayer
and worn
with thanks.

THOMAS GOODWIN

46

Sweetest Blessings

If you were given everything you wanted right away, would you value those things? Or would they become commonplace after the novelty had worn off? When you don't work hard for something you want but you receive it anyway, the feeling of enjoyment and accomplishment are often absent, and you don't enjoy the success the way you would have had you been working for the same goal. When you've waited patiently to see the seeds you've planted begin to grow, it's much more exciting and fulfilling!

The things that we long for, pray for, and work for are infinitely more valuable to us once we have them. Those are things to be cherished, guarded, and so very thankful for.

Remind yourself of your sweetest blessings. Make a list of the things in your life that you hoped and prayed for and received. What do those things mean to you now?

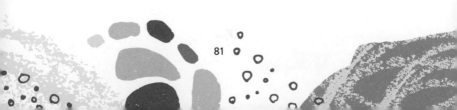

Never doubt that a small group of thoughtful, committed citizens can change the world. Indeed, it is the only thing that ever has.

MARGARET MEAD

47

The Friendly Fridge

When Selma Raven and Sara Allen wanted to help others in their neighborhood in the Bronx, they bought an old refrigerator on Craigslist and opened the Friendly Fridge.[10] A local building owner agreed to let them plug the fridge in outside of his restaurant, and Selma and Sara filled it with free, fresh food for anyone to take.

The system is simple. Anyone can leave what they have. Anyone can take what they need. When it first opened, word spread and donations began to appear each day. Even today, a local fruit vendor will drop off fruit, deli owners on the block will donate sandwiches, and neighbors will bring by vegetables from their gardens. At the end of every day, Selma, Sara, and their friends clean out anything old, sanitize the fridge, and refill it with donations and food they buy to supplement community offerings.

"As someone special in my life once said, 'No one should go hungry,'" says Raven. "And thanks to this amazing neighborhood, we can all help."

Who, being loved, is poor?

OSCAR WILDE

48

Be the First to Love

If you can name even one person who loves you, then you have a lot to be grateful for. At the end of the day, that's what we all want: someone to love us and someone we can love in return.

We all want to be seen and loved, just as we are. That is what drives us, more than anything else. Of course, most of us are also terrified that we will never find someone who truly sees us and loves us, including all of our bad habits, flaws, and insecurities!

The secret to finding that kind of love is to love others that way. Our instincts tell us to hold back until we are sure the recipient of our love also loves us, but that doesn't make sense. For unconditional love to grow, someone has to take the chance to love first.

Let it be you.

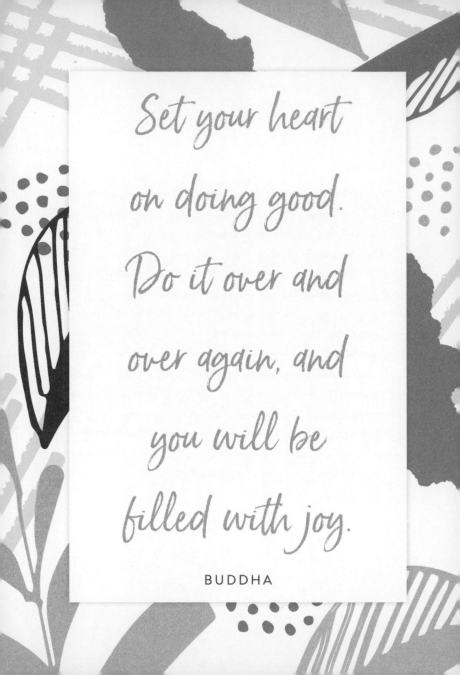

Set your heart on doing good. Do it over and over again, and you will be filled with joy.

BUDDHA

49

Do Good

Doing good won't get you very far if you only do it because you feel like you *have* to or it's the right thing to do. Sure, you might help people, but you won't have nearly the same impact as if your heart were really in it.

No rule says you have to volunteer at a soup kitchen if you hate working with food or to work for a humane society if you are allergic to cats. Doing good shouldn't be drudgery.

Think about what you genuinely love to do, and then find an organization that needs those things. Love graphic design? Offer to create a new website for a charity. Are you a knitter? Find organizations that provide scarves for refugees. Skilled at math? Volunteer to help tutor local students.

There are a million ways to help. Take the time to find your perfect fit. When you find the right way to make a difference, it won't feel like work. It will feel like joy.

Above all, keep
loving one
another earnestly,
since love covers
a multitude
of sins.

1 PETER 4:8 ESV

50

Keep Loving Others

We all sin and fall short of the glory of God. We are blessed beyond measure that God loves us so much that He has forgiven our sins. That kind of life-changing love should be experienced by everyone. That's where we come in.

As we walk through our lives, we have opportunities each day to show God-inspired love to everyone we meet. God waits to meet us in those moments, to supplement the love we show with His own. He wants us to shower our communities with grace and care, to help the helpless, and to strengthen the weak.

That can be difficult to do. We all have busy lives and responsibilities that can get in the way. But God will always make up the difference when we feel like we don't have the energy, time, patience, or the courage to love like He does.

51

A Nation of Volunteers

This nation will remain the land of the free only
so long as it is the home of the brave.

ELMER DAVIS

For so many of us, the coronavirus pandemic was the first time we had been asked, as a nation, to make a collective sacrifice for the greater good. But it certainly wasn't the first time in our history.

During World War II, more than six million citizens volunteered for military service. Millions of women bravely took up the jobs their husbands had left behind in factories to produce tanks, torpedoes, and other weapons. In addition, rations imposed on meat, sugar, and medicines meant that every American personally sacrificed. Women and children grew victory gardens and bought war bonds. Our country came together to defeat a horrible evil, and all of those sacrifices added up. The contributions Americans made turned the tide of the war, leading to victory.

Of course, that is only one example of many. Americans have always been willing to do what was needed, be it staying home and wearing masks or stepping up to serve, so that lives could be saved and good could prevail. And that is something to be proud of.

52

A New Home

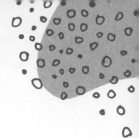

Home is the nicest word there is.

LAURA INGALLS WILDER

Tony had never had a home he could count on.[11] He was given up for adoption as a baby, bounced around the foster system, and was finally adopted when he was four years old. But when he was eleven, his adoptive parents left him at a hospital in Charlotte, North Carolina, and never returned for him.

Scared, alone, and feeling utterly unlovable, Tony needed somewhere to go until his situation could be sorted out. A social worker called up Peter, who had already been a foster parent. Peter agreed to take Tony in and vowed to help Tony overcome the trauma of being abandoned.

"I was crying," Peter told *Good Morning America*. "I thought, 'Who would do that?'" Tony moved in with Peter and finally found his first real home. Peter officially adopted Tony a few years later. In the process, both Peter and Tony found the family they had always longed for in each other.

Abolish fear,

and every man

and woman

is an orator

and an artist.

ELBERT HUBBARD

5 3
Fear Not

Is there something that you've always wanted to do but just can't seem to get done? Maybe you are always too busy? Or it just never seems like the right time? Fear is always happy to hand us a million excuses to keep from taking a risk and chasing our dreams.

You may not even consciously recognize that most of your excuses come from a place of fear, but they do. Fear of failure, embarrassment, or even just putting yourself out there. Fear is so tricky because it disguises itself as countless other things. But when you strip away all of the excuses, there is your dream, still waiting for you to become braver than your fears.

It's your life and you only get one chance to live it, so don't let fear hold you back from making it what you want.

Gratitude is
the fairest
blossom
which
springs from
the soul.

HENRY WARD BEECHER

54

Be Thankful in the Present

Take a few minutes to stop and give thanks for everything you have. Nothing is too small to consider and be thankful for. Even if your life is not what you hoped it would be or feels heavy right now, it is still a good life. You are blessed in so many ways.

With our eyes on the future, we can forget to look in the present and see the goodness all around us. It is there, but you may have become blind to your blessings because you see them every day and take them for granted. That's happened to each of us at times, and sometimes you need to shake things up to see how good you have it.

Make a list of those blessings. Then consider how difficult your life would be without them. Is there something you could do today to reach out and bless someone who doesn't have everything you do?

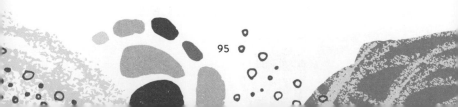

I am beginning
to learn that it is
the sweet, simple
things of life
which are the real
ones after all.

LAURA INGALLS WILDER

55

Make Some Lasagna!

A pan of homemade lasagna may seem ordinary, but Michelle Brenner turned lasagna into hope when she made more than one thousand pans of it for neighbors in need during the COVID-19 pandemic.[12]

When Michelle was furloughed from her retail job because of the lockdown, she made herself a pan of the ultimate comfort food—her grandmother's lasagna. Then she decided to see if anyone else could use a good meal. Michelle took her government stimulus check and used it to buy ingredients for more lasagna. She posted her offer for free lasagna to anyone who could come pick it up, and then she started cooking. She made more than twelve hundred pans of lasagna for families in her community over the course of the spring, including delivering pans to essential workers at the local hospital, police and fire departments, and the prison.

"The world as we know it is falling apart, but my two little hands are capable of making a difference," Michelle explained. "I can't change the world, but I can make lasagna." Her secret ingredient? Love.

Great works do
not always come
our way, but every
moment presents us
with opportunities
to do little ones
with excellence.

ST. FRANCIS DE SALES

56

Celebrate All Jobs

Sanitation workers Saul Scruggs and Keon Richardson were shocked when they rounded a corner in their garbage truck as part of their regular route and found themselves in the middle of a party thrown to honor them.[13] The residents of one Miami Beach neighborhood had come together to thank and honor the men who do such essential work for them.

Signs, balloons, and small gifts gave the street a festive atmosphere as neighbors took turns expressing their gratitude. One lady told a story of how Saul had helped her go through her trash for forty-five minutes searching for her missing wedding ring. Another shared how Saul had waited for an ambulance with a neighbor for more than an hour so he wouldn't have to be alone. Even the Miami Beach mayor came out to show his appreciation.

Trash pickup can be a dirty job, but it is essential. Is there someone essential to your life whom you want to thank today?

No one is
useless in
this world
who lightens
the burdens
of another.

CHARLES DICKENS

57

No One Does Anything Truly Alone

Each of us is different and deals with different challenges and circumstances that might be hidden from casual observers. If you live with a disability, daily pain, a chronic illness, or mental health issues, it can be seriously challenging to commit to too much. It can be frustrating to see others out in the world leaving their mark and working for change when you feel stuck, hampered by your limitations.

Luckily, just being there for your friends and family to listen to them, cry with them, and celebrate with them can make a big difference in their lives. Even the most hardcore activists and change warriors need supporters. Your encouragement and advice contribute so much to their success, just like the encouragement of your family and friends has contributed to your achievements.

No one does anything truly alone. Don't forget that.

No star is ever
lost we once
have seen, we
always may be
what we might
have been.

ADELAIDE ANNE PROCTER

58

What Are You Waiting For?

Are you happy with your life? Are you proud of who you are and what you do? Are you living the life you've always pictured? If your answer to any of those questions was no, what are you waiting for?

The perfect job or the spouse of your dreams isn't just going to fall in your lap one day. You won't be accepted to your dream school if you don't apply. You can't just walk up to board an airplane to an exotic destination without booking a ticket.

Life isn't something that happens *to you*. Life is something that *you create* with every choice and decision you make. Settling for what you have right now is a choice. Going after something better is another one. Whatever you choose, remember that you are the only one who can make your life into what you want it to be. It's never too late to make new choices.

Unless someone like you cares a whole awful lot, nothing is going to get better. It's not.

DR. SEUSS

59

Love with Abandon

Children can teach us a lot about what it means to love with abandon. Five-year-old Michael had longed to be adopted.[14] When he finally found his forever family, he knew just whom he wanted to celebrate with: his kindergarten class.

That's right, Michael's entire kindergarten class came to his adoption hearing. They made heart-shaped signs and each of them stood before the judge to explain what they loved about Michael. "We began the school year as a family. Family doesn't have to be DNA, because family is support and love," explained his teacher.

When the adoption was official, the whole crowd erupted in cheers, proving to Michael just how much he was loved by everyone in both of his chosen families.

Far away there in
the sunshine are my
highest aspirations.
I cannot reach them,
but I can look up
and see their beauty,
believe in them,
and try to follow
where they lead.

LOUISA MAY ALCOTT

60

No Dream Is Too Wild

Goals and dreams are beautiful things to have. We all need things to reach for, to motivate us to be bold and brave and take leaps of faith from time to time.

There really is no dream that is too big. In fact, some of people's wildest, biggest dreams have come true in spectacular ways. Think of the Wright brothers flying the first airplane or Alexander Graham Bell making his first phone call. Once upon a time, the very idea of an airplane or telephone seemed impossible. Now, we can't imagine our lives without them.

Is there a dream you've been discounting because it seems too wild? It isn't. Nothing is really impossible; it just hasn't been achieved *yet*. So why not you?

61

Learn About a New Culture

Who gives himself with his alms feeds three,—
Himself, his hungering neighbor, and me.

JAMES RUSSELL LOWELL

The world is so much bigger than any of us truly realize. There are so many different cultures, a boundless number of beautiful traditions, and such a wide variety of perspectives. And it's a good thing too because life would be terribly boring if we were all the same!

Most of us only see a tiny slice of the world in our lifetimes. Even if we are able to travel, we can't fully understand the needs of someone living in another country when we are just visiting.

The best way you can try to connect with a different worldview is to read. Find a nonfiction book written by a woman from Japan or a collection of poems by a man living in Sri Lanka. Delve into fiction from Belgium or short stories from South Africa. The more you read, the more you will be able to love those people as you do your own neighbors.

62

Social Media Detox

There's no Wi-Fi in the mountains, but
you'll find a better connection.

The internet is not always a kind place. Scrolling through social media can make you feel inadequate, clickbait articles can rile up your temper, and comments sections can leave you saddened. Every once in a while it's a good idea to go on a digital detox from all of that noise and nonsense.

Turn off your phone, grab some friends, and head up to a cabin for a weekend of rustic living. Head out to your garden and tend the flowers. Pick up your favorite book and revisit old friends in its pages. Take your dog for a hike and enjoy all the beauty around you. Get in the kitchen and make something delicious from scratch. Put on some good music and laze the day away in a hammock in your yard.

Turn off your Wi-Fi and focus on the life that's right in front of you. It does still exist, even if it doesn't get posted online!

True happiness
is to enjoy
the present,
without anxious
dependence
upon the future.

SENECA

63

Enjoy Life Right Now

It's nice to be prepared, to walk into a room feeling confident and ready to take on whatever comes your way. Looking ahead and planning for potential pitfalls and issues will make life go more smoothly and help you feel calmer when unexpected challenges pop up. But there is just no way to be completely prepared for everything.

Even if you spent all of your time imagining scenarios and coming up with plans and work-arounds, you couldn't possibly cover everything that can and might happen in your life. If all you think about are the bad things that could happen, you will become blind to all of the wonderful things happening all around you.

Don't let your fears of the what-ifs stop you from enjoying the right now.

Blessed are they who see beautiful things in humble places where other people see nothing.

CAMILLE PISSARRO

64

Beauty in Broken Places

Beauty is in the eye of the beholder. When your heart and mind are focused on all you lack and all the ways life is unfair, you will only see a world that is as bleak and bitter as you feel. But when your heart is full of love and your mind is focused on doing good, you will see beauty in even the most broken of places.

Loveliness is all around you if you have the heart to find it. As you go about your day, be mindful; search for the beauty of the everyday and let it bolster your thoughts, making them beautiful too.

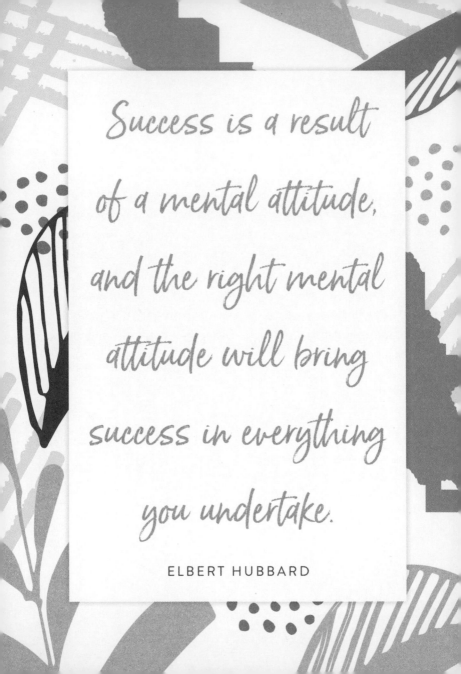

Success is a result of a mental attitude, and the right mental attitude will bring success in everything you undertake.

ELBERT HUBBARD

65

Your Thoughts Have Power

Our thoughts have power. When we focus on the good in life, we will notice more and more good things around us to be grateful for and to celebrate. However, when our thoughts are filled with storm clouds, all we will be able to see is the dirty, messy, and ugly.

If you struggle to keep your thoughts positive, try choosing a mantra, a short, simple phrase that you can repeat to yourself anytime you feel your thoughts sliding into negative territory. Your mantra can be anything, but here are a few examples you can try until you settle on one of your own:

- Today is going to be a good day.
- I am grateful for all the beauty in my life.
- I choose joy today.

I feel my heart glow with an enthusiasm which elevates me to heaven, for nothing contributes so much to tranquillize the mind as a steady purpose—a point on which the soul may fix its intellectual eye.

MARY SHELLEY

66

What Are Your Passions?

You have something amazing to contribute to this world, something that only you can bring to the table. Have you found it yet? Start now.

Make a list of all of your strengths. Make another list of everything you love doing. Now make another list of things that you care deeply about. And another of things that break your heart. Look at those lists altogether. What do they have in common? Where do they overlap? Do you see a theme emerging?

Follow those commonalities. Do your research. How can you put your skills and passions to work for the things that you care about, fixing the things that break your heart? Once you can answer that, you'll have your purpose.

Love one another with brotherly affection. Outdo one another in showing honor.

ROMANS 12:10 ESV

67

You Are Able to Love Others

Following Jesus is not for the faint of heart. Jesus doesn't let us sing some hymns and go to Bible study each week and say we're done. He challenges us to do more and be better. He dares us to be bolder and braver and to love harder. He urges us to step outside of our comfort zones to care for one another in the middle of our messy lives and emotions.

Jesus was human too. He knows how we feel and what our weaknesses are. But He also knows what we are capable of. He doesn't ask us to do anything that we *can't* do. So when the Bible tells us to "love one another" and to "outdo one another in showing honor," we can be confident that those are things we can absolutely do.

How will you rise to the challenge today?

68

Live as You Preach

What you do speaks so loudly that I
cannot hear what you say.

RALPH WALDO EMERSON

Our world is so noisy these days. Social media infiltrates every aspect of our lives, bringing the words and opinions of family, friends, and even strangers into our living rooms, kitchens, and bedrooms. The comments sections of articles bleed over into family time, and the griping of annoyed neighbors slips into bed with us as we scroll through our phones before falling asleep.

In the midst of all this noise, words can become hollow and empty. Anyone can say the right thing, but the truth of someone's character and convictions comes out loudly and clearly in their actions. If you are talking the talk, you better be walking the walk. If you aren't, then it doesn't matter how big your platform is; eventually, people will stop listening.

If you are passionate about an issue, all the promises of love and light and prayers don't amount to anything if you aren't following those words up with action. If it matters to you, show up.

69

Help Everyone

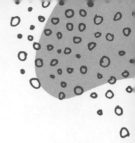

In everything I did, I showed you that by this kind
of hard work we must help the weak, remembering
the words the Lord Jesus himself said: "It is
more blessed to give than to receive."

ACTS 20:35

Jesus calls us all so clearly to love and help others. He doesn't mince words or speak in riddles. He doesn't suggest we only help people who agree with us or who look like us. He doesn't let us off the hook because we already helped some other people some other time. He doesn't give guidelines for determining which of the weak are more deserving than others. No, Jesus calls us to help *everyone* in need.

Is there a group that you feel resistant to help? People who you don't think deserve your money or your time? We all have blind spots and stumbling blocks. But Jesus' love for each and every one of us is bigger than our blind spots. Take some time to talk this over with God. Pray for His guidance and for Him to work in your heart to help you want to help *all* people in need.

Laughter is

a sunbeam

of the soul.

THOMAS MANN

70

Laugh More Than a Little

Do yourself a favor today. When you start to feel down or discouraged, lie down on your floor. Get comfy and place your hand on your stomach. Take a few deep, slow breaths. Now, smile. Even if it feels strange, hold that smile for thirty seconds. Once you've done that, laugh. Choose your silliest, fakest laugh, and really go for it. Laugh as long and hard as you can. Don't be surprised if you really do start genuinely laughing. After all, to be fake laughing on your floor in the middle of the afternoon is pretty hilarious!

Your body doesn't know the difference between a fake smile and a real smile or a fake laugh and a real laugh.[15] Smiles and laughter reduce the levels of cortisol (also known as the stress hormones) in your body, all while stimulating the production of endorphins, which are feel-good hormones. Once you feel a little less stressed, you may find yourself smiling for real.

Rest

and be

thankful.

WILLIAM WORDSWORTH

71

Rest Is Essential

None of us can work around the clock. Rest is essential to keeping your spirits up and to giving you enough energy to get back to work again.

It is not selfish or lazy to prioritize rest. You can only do so much in a day, week, or month before you run out of steam. Pushing yourself to keep going past the point of exhaustion will only lead to burnout. And once you burn out, regaining your energy and passion is a long journey.

Caring for yourself with love and tenderness as you go is far easier. Rest when you grow weary. Eat good food when you are hungry. Take time out for joy and connection. Count your blessings and appreciate the life you have now and the journey you are on before you pick your work up again and continue.

72

Love Yourself

Self-trust is the first secret of success.

RALPH WALDO EMERSON

Loving yourself—truly loving yourself—lays a firm foundation for building the life that you want. Of course, even the most confident among us struggle sometimes when they look in the mirror. We all have weaknesses and flaws, areas we're ashamed of or embarrassed by. But sometimes those things aren't really flaws at all; we've just been looking at them the wrong way.

Today take a few moments and try to reframe your imperfections. You aren't combative; you are filled with passion. You aren't bossy; you're a natural leader. You aren't too much; you are just still finding the people who can handle you. You aren't a crybaby; you are deeply empathetic. You aren't a softy; you have a heart full of love. You aren't naïve; you believe in the goodness of people.

You are better, stronger, and more beautiful than you give yourself credit for. Let's start believing that!

73

Where Is Your Home?

As much as I converse with sages and heroes, they
have very little of my love and admiration. I long
for rural and domestic scene, for the warbling
of birds and the prattling of my children.

JOHN ADAMS

They say, "Home is where the heart is." But that home isn't
necessarily a place. Home is wherever your family is, wherever
the people who love you best are waiting for you.

Your family might be your husband and kids or your mom
and dad or your brothers and sisters, or it may be a family that
you've chosen made up of dear friends and trusted mentors.
It is with your family that you can let down your guard and be
open and vulnerable to learning and growing. It is when you are
surrounded by love that you feel safe enough to take a risk.
Families encourage us to fly but also give us a safe place to land.

Call your family today. Even if you are far from home, you
are never far from their love.

No work is insignificant.
All labor that uplifts
humanity has dignity and
importance and should
be undertaken with
painstaking excellence.

MARTIN LUTHER KING JR.

74

Be Grateful for Essential Workers

As we all discovered during the COVID-19 pandemic, a lot of essential workers do jobs that people tend to take for granted. We all expect that there will be someone to ring up our groceries, clean our offices, and drive our buses. But how often do we take the time to say thank you and really see and connect with the people doing those jobs?

There are no small jobs, not in the grand scheme of things. These essential workers hold together our access to food, safe transportation, and disease prevention, whether we acknowledge them or not. Let's not forget that again. They deserve our respect, admiration, and gratitude.

Take the time today to say thank you to the essential workers who help make your life easier and safer every day.

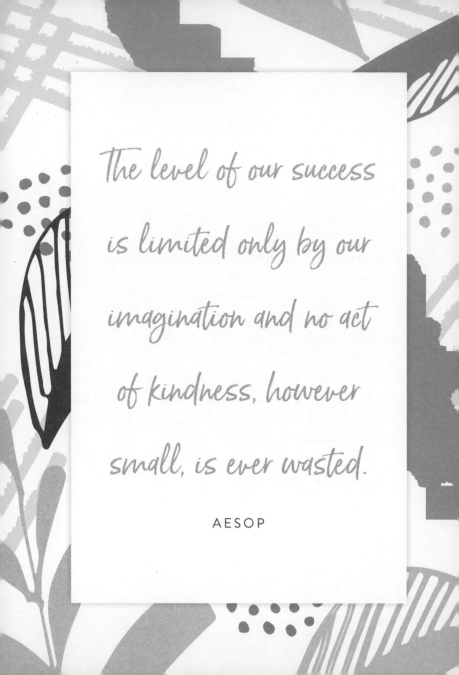

The level of our success
is limited only by our
imagination and no act
of kindness, however
small, is ever wasted.

AESOP

75

Delight Someone Today

James Anthony had worked at Hickerson Elementary in Tullahoma, Tennessee, for more than fifteen years when he got the surprise of his life.[16] On the partially deaf custodian's sixtieth birthday, he was called into a kindergarten class, where the children were waiting to surprise him.

When James walked in, the children immediately began to sing and sign "Happy Birthday" in American Sign Language. Completely caught by surprise, James was nearly moved to tears by the gesture. It meant so much to him that the kindergartners and their teachers had worked for weeks to master the signs to the song with the help of the school nurse. The kids were delighted they could put a smile on the face of the caring custodian who was always so kind to them.

Is there someone who you can delight with a simple gesture like that today?

76

Help Others See

They might not need me; but they might. I'll
let my head be just in sight; a smile as small as
mine might be precisely their necessity.

EMILY DICKINSON

Imagine walking through the world blind. How difficult would it be to navigate pedestrian traffic or shop for groceries with no help?

Be My Eyes[17] is an app that was developed to help in those situations. More than three million sighted volunteers lend their eyes to solve tasks big and small to help blind or low-vision users lead more independent lives. With the app, a user can be connected with a volunteer through a video call to get help with anything from checking an expiration date to navigating new surroundings.

Be My Eyes was founded by Hans Jørgen Wiberg, who is visually impaired himself. He explained, "It's my hope that by helping each other as an online community, Be My Eyes will make a big difference in the everyday lives of blind people all over the world." It took a lot of vision to come up with a solution to this problem, and it took even more heart for volunteers to jump at the chance to help when needed.

77

Keep Trying

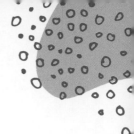

Strength and growth come only through
continuous effort and struggle.

NAPOLEON HILL

Success is almost always preceded by a long list of failures. No
one is great at something the first time they do it. It takes time
and hard work to learn something new or to create something
out of nothing.

You will have setbacks and failures and get sidetracked over
and over again. But a failure is only really a failure if you refuse
to try again. If you get back up and start again, that failure
becomes a lesson, a learning experience. Lesson by lesson, you
will figure things out and eventually succeed.

Resilient people are willing to throw themselves off the
cliff again and again, knowing they will fall. But every time they
get back up and do it again, they try something a little different
and fall a little less spectacularly—until one day they fly.

We make a living by what we get. We make a life by what we give.

WINSTON CHURCHILL

78

Offer Your Help

Derrick Campana started out building prosthetic devices for people, but it wasn't until a client brought in her black Labrador retriever, Charles, for help that Derrick found his true purpose.[18] He created a device to help Charles and realized he needed to switch gears. The next year Derrick founded Animal OrthoCare, and his company has since helped more than twenty thousand animals regain mobility with their devices.

Derrick treats the usual pets such as cats, dogs, and rabbits, but he also treats other animals, including elephants, sheep, goats, llamas, and camels. Thanks to Derrick's tireless efforts, these animals are able to walk and run again, filling the world with just a little more joy.

The best part
of beauty is
that which
no picture can
express.

FRANCIS BACON

79
We Are Adaptable

We are all unique. All of us, like trees that grow around twisted and angled obstacles and contort, our experiences change and transform us, and we grow to create something perfectly imperfect and beautiful. In fact, none of us would have quite such beautiful spirits if it weren't for the challenges and obstacles that required us to bend and twist and adapt. What makes you so incredibly beautiful is what other don't see on the outside, but what is inside of you.

The strongest trees are the ones that can bow instead of break, and that's true of people too. Flexibility, grace, and the desire to survive and thrive allows you to bend when the highest winds blow but then twist and stretch to reach the sunshine on dark days. Each crook and curve is a testament to your resilience, and you should wear them proudly.

A good friend
is like a four-
leaf clover: hard
to find and
lucky to have.

IRISH PROVERB

80

Man's Best Friend

It can be difficult to teach an old dog new tricks, but no dog is too old to be man's best friend. In San Francisco, the Cuddle Club helps senior dogs make new friends with community seniors.[19] Several times a month, the Cuddle Club, which was started by the Muttville Senior Dog Rescue, holds events where senior citizens gather to pet and play with senior rescue dogs.

Each of the dogs is seven years or older and not as likely to be adopted by families looking for puppies. The Cuddle Club ensures that these sweet dogs get plenty of attention and love. The human group members love the events too. At the end of each session, the seniors take the dogs out for a walk, and it's not unusual to see a small dog riding along on someone's walker. Many participants find a match at the events and end up adopting a new best friend to take home with them.

A hero is no braver than an ordinary man, but he is brave five minutes longer.

RALPH WALDO EMERSON

81

Real-Life Superheroes

It would be awfully nice if superheroes, with their mythical powers, were really around to swoop in and save the day when needed. Luckily, there are heroes in every community who are pretty super.

When members of the Aurora SWAT heard that some superhero fans at the Children's Hospital Colorado needed cheering up, they decided to do something about it.[20] Officers dressed up as different fan-favorite superheroes, such as Batman, Superman, Captain America, Spiderman, and Iron Man, and then rappelled down the sides of the hospital. Each officer stopped at different windows, delighting the pint-sized patients inside. The glimpse of their favorite characters gave the kids hope and encouragement to keep fighting, and that's about as super as you can get!

It's been my experience that you can nearly always enjoy things if you make up your mind firmly that you will.

L. M. MONTGOMERY

82

In a Bad Season

We all have to do things we'd rather not in life. We get stuck in a situation and the only way out is to go through it. Or we have to do something unpleasant to get to something we want to do. Maybe we must choose the best of several bad choices for a season.

Whatever the reason, when you feel stuck, you can wallow in frustration and discouragement or you can decide to make the best of the situation. If you choose to see the humor, fun, and opportunities where you are, being stuck won't feel nearly so sticky. You will be more open to learning and growing and more willing to take risks and try new things. In fact, you might even find that you enjoy yourself while you wait for the next opportunity or the season to change!

83

The Story of Your Life

You can't do anything about the length of your life, but
you can do something about its width and depth.

H. L. MENCKEN

You are the one writing the story of your life. You may not be
able to choose all of the plot points, but you get to decide if
yours is a story of triumph and joy, grit and grace, or despair
and destruction. If you were telling your story right now, what
kind of story would it be?

If you aren't happy with your story right now, it's not too
late. Every day you have the chance to write new pages, and the
ending certainly hasn't been written yet. There is still time to
add new chapters, tweak the plot, and mix up the characters.
But to do all of that, you have to take an active hand in its
creation. Decide what you want and write something you can
be proud of.

84

Climb to the Peak

If we always helped one another, no one would need luck.

SOPHOCLES

No one gets anywhere in life alone. Some of us get a lot of help and others get very little. Some of us start halfway up the mountain and others start miles away from base camp. None of us can pick the circumstances we're born into, or we'd all pick loving, supportive families with plenty of money and resources. But we all have the chance to help someone else along.

Even if you work harder than anyone else, it might take you longer to reach the peak because you had to start from the bottom. If you are someone who reached the peak quickly because you had a head start and all the right gear, why not try to make the path easier for those still climbing? Your helping hand could be the difference that makes someone else's climb possible.

Imagine if we all worked to make the climb a little easier for the people to come after us. Eventually, just about everyone would be able to reach the peak, and we'd all be treated to a view of a new world waiting just for us.

Look not mournfully into the past. It comes not back again. Wisely improve the present. It is thine.

HENRY WADSWORTH LONGFELLOW

85

Live in the Present

We are often so focused on the future or lost reminiscing about the past that we forget to be present in the present. It's so easy to romanticize things that have already happened or to paint the future in a rosy glow of possibility, but all we really have is right here and now.

What's done is done and we are not promised the future; however, today is yours to do what you will with it. All those things you've been putting off for some hazy day when the time is right? The time is right now. Today is the day to start doing them.

When we choose to be present in the here and now, focusing on *being* instead of planning, life becomes more vivid and vibrant, more alive with the promise that anything can happen and that we will be ready to grab hold of the opportunity when it presents itself.

I may not always be there with you, but I will always be there for you.

86
Never Too Far Away

When we are far away from the ones we love most, it can feel lonely. We all remember the first time we were far away from home and those aching feelings of longing for the comforting familiar and the warm glow of the love we'd always known.

It gets easier to be apart with time. You develop your own routine, meet new friends, and create a new home wherever you are, but it doesn't make the missing go away. Whether they are an hour away or across the country, know that the people you love miss you too.

Stay connected with frequent calls and video chats, or try writing good old-fashioned letters so you can look forward to opening the mailbox. And never underestimate the power of a care package filled with homemade goodies. Brownies are an excellent way to say, "I love you."

"For I know the plans I have for you," declares the LORD, "plans to prosper you and not to harm you, plans to give you hope and a future."

JEREMIAH 29:11

87

His Plans Are Better

Sometimes we face things that seem far too big to overcome, but we were never meant to face them alone. God walks beside us every step of the way.

Despite having seen the miraculous ways that God works in the world, we have a tendency to think of God as if He were one of us, with our limitations and incomplete knowledge. But God is so much bigger than we can even fathom. He sees the complete picture, while we see only fragments. He makes impossible things possible. He is more than big enough to face our biggest challenges and obstacles. All we have to do is ask.

God has big plans for you, and His plans are always good ones, far better than anything you can imagine for yourself. So as you face down the tough stuff, ask for God's help, and then hold tightly both to Him and His promise that good things are coming for you.

It's good to be

blessed. It's

better to be

a blessing.

88

Don't Hide Your Shine

Don't ever hide your shine. The world needs your light. You are a blessing to someone out there, and, very likely, many someones! Your kind words, caring deeds, good work, and encouragement brighten the days of those people and inspire them to treat others well too.

Even if you don't always see it, your life makes a difference in the lives of the people you know. Forgetting how much influence you have can be easy, but there isn't a single person who doesn't influence others regularly. It's up to you to choose whether you want to leave anger and frustration in your wake or love and kindness.

Every smile, every word spoken with wisdom, every caring conversation, and every thoughtful deed adds up over time to create your legacy. Keep working to make it one you are proud of.

"To love him with all your heart, with all your understanding and with all your strength, and to love your neighbor as yourself is more important than all burnt offerings and sacrifices."

MARK 12:33

89

The Two Greatest Commandments

God's greatest commandments to us are to love Him and to love our neighbors as ourselves. It all boils down to living a life overflowing with love, to treating others with the same kindness and care that Jesus demonstrated for us. So how does something so simple become so complicated?

In truth, it's still that simple. Our disagreements about politics, our rules about who can and can't do what, and our insistence that some people must surely be better than others just don't hold up when viewed through the lens of love.

Choose love today. Ask God to lend you His vision. As you interact with each person you meet, ask yourself how you can love them like Jesus. And then do it. You'll find your heart warming toward even the most seemingly unlovable people when you do your best to see them through Jesus' eyes.

All men's

miseries

derive from not

being able to

sit in a quiet

room alone.

BLAISE PASCAL

90

Enjoy a Quiet Season

Each life is made up of different seasons. Some of those seasons are filled with vibrant conversations, unhindered laughter, and companionship. Other seasons are quieter and marked by time spent alone. When you find yourself in a quiet season, remind yourself that there is a difference between being alone and being lonely.

There are abundant blessings to be found in having a season to yourself. Having the time to examine your priorities and the freedom to chase your wildest dreams and then build a life that you are passionate about is special. Not having to answer to anyone if you want to travel on a whim or spend an entire day lounging in bed is a luxury that you may not be able to indulge in during other seasons. Having fewer distractions means that you can focus on building up friendships or giving back to your community.

No season lasts forever, so cherish the blessings unique to where you are right now while you have them.

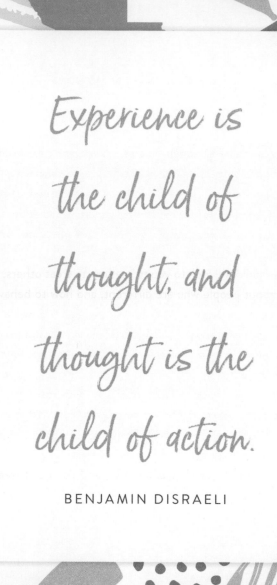

Experience is the child of thought, and thought is the child of action.

BENJAMIN DISRAELI

91

An Example for Your Child

Are you a parent? Or maybe you hope to be someday? Raising kids is such an incredible job. You get to see a person grow from a tiny baby into a fully formed human before your very eyes. It's also challenging. Your role as a parent is to teach that developing person how to be a functioning member of society before they become an adult. No pressure, right?

Your child will look to you to see how to treat others, how to talk about people who are different, and how to behave as a member of your community. Even if you tell them all of the right things, if you aren't walking the walk, they will notice. Your actions send a stronger message to your kids than hours of lectures ever could.

Show your child what unconditional love looks like. Pour out kindness to your neighbors. Celebrate differences and treat others with respect. Be someone whom your community can count on to do the right thing.

Start now—your child is watching and you don't want to let them down.

92

What Makes Someone Lovely?

And now here is my secret, a very simple secret:
it is only with the heart that one can see rightly;
what is essential is invisible to the eye.

ANTOINE DE SAINT-EXUPÉRY

The real beauty of a person lies in what fills her heart. An attractive face doesn't make someone lovely. A heart filled with honesty, kindness, love, compassion, sympathy, perseverance, and a genuine desire to do good makes even the plainest of us stunning beauties.

Anyone in your life who values looks over substance or the flash of money and power over a developed character isn't worth keeping around. If they only assign worth based on things they can see, there is nothing you will ever be able to do to show them your true value. Surround yourself with people who really *see* you, right down to the depths of your soul, and know exactly what a treasure they have found in your friendship and love.

93

Show Jesus to Your Community

Let us hold fast the confession of our hope
without wavering. . . . And let us consider how to
stir up one another to love and good works.

HEBREWS 10:23–24 ESV

The early Christian church was founded as a way for believers to come together to encourage one another, discuss the teachings of Jesus, and find ways to be salt and light in their communities. Believers didn't meet together just to be seen or because it was the *thing* to do. They went because they were on fire for Jesus. They wanted desperately to become more like Him, and they needed reminders and encouragement to stay on the right path.

They became known for their good deeds and the love they showed everyone—especially for those on whom society had turned their backs. They didn't just give money each week and call it good. They went out into their communities and got their hands dirty. And then they challenged each other to do more. Let's show our communities what the love of Jesus looks like.

When one door
closes another
always opens, but
we usually look so
long, so intently and
so sorrowfully upon
the closed door that
we do not see the
one that has opened.

94

The Sun Still Rises

There are losses so profound that it feels like the world has stopped spinning, that surely time has stilled at the exact moment the loss occurred. Because how can the sun continue to rise and set or the tides go in and out or children go to school when your heart has been frozen with grief?

No matter how all-consuming your grief is, the sun will set and rise again. It might take a long time (and there is no set amount of time it *should* take), but eventually you won't feel so stuck. The sense of loss will never go away entirely, but you will learn to live with your grief. Spring will come again. Flowers will bloom. You will laugh and love again.

Nothing will ever be the same, but you will find that there is still beauty in the world and that life is still worth living.

Do the difficult things
while they are easy
and do the great things
while they are small.
A journey of a thousand
miles must begin
with a single step.

LAO TZU

95
Start with One Small Step

When you have a big dream or a lofty goal, it can feel overwhelming or intimidating when you think of just how much has to be done. Feel anxious just reading that? It's okay. Take a deep breath. Now say this out loud to yourself: I don't have to do all of this at once.

The best way to approach these big things is to break them down into smaller goals, and then break them down again into smaller actions. Keep breaking things down until you have a list of actionable steps that are much easier to achieve. Take time every day to complete one or two steps, and before you know it your goal will be in sight!

Throw off your
worries when
you throw off
your clothes
at night.

NAPOLÉON BONAPARTE

96

Rest at Night

If you want to be able to do good in the world day after day, then rest is essential. When the world feels scary or you are in a situation completely out of your control, it can be easy to feel like you have to watch the news constantly or spend every moment trying to make plans. But all that does is leave you exhausted, anxious, and too emotionally depleted to face the challenges in front of you.

As you lie in bed tonight, try this simple exercise. Take deep, slow breaths. With each breath in, picture one of your worries in your mind. Then when you breathe out, picture that worry being released from your mind and body. Imagine each worry drifting up into the night sky. Repeat this until your mind is clear and you can relax—at least for the night.

97
Do What You Can

Whatever I have tried to do in life, I have tried with all my
heart to do well; that whatever I have devoted myself to,
I have devoted myself to completely; that in great aims
and in small, I have always been thoroughly in earnest.

CHARLES DICKENS

It is a myth that you can do it all. You can do anything you put
your mind to, certainly, but you can't do everything, and you
definitely can't do everything all at once! At some point in life
you are going to have to choose what to pursue and what to let
go of. If you try to do it all, you won't be able to do any of it well.

Some of us seem to be born knowing what we want out of
life, and some of us take our whole lives trying to figure it out.
But the truth is that each of us has only so much time, so it is
imperative that we prioritize the things that matter most to us
and let go of the things that don't. Devote yourself to the goals
and dreams you have burning inside of you, and you won't be
disappointed.

98

Speak with Kindness

She opens her mouth with wisdom, and the
teaching of kindness is on her tongue.

PROVERBS 31:26 ESV

The much-lauded woman of Proverbs 31 sometimes gets a bad rap for being a little *too* perfect. However, for all the wonderful things said about her, the most important is that she knows when to speak up and when to keep her peace—and when she does speak, she does so with kindness. If you were her neighbor, you might feel envious of or even a little resentful toward her, but it's more likely that you'd want to be her friend because of her kindness. It's pretty difficult to feel any anger or jealousy about someone who is unfailingly kind.

What if all of your words were spoken with kindness? How would that change the way you speak to others and to yourself?

There is a sacredness in tears. They are not a mark of weakness, but of power. They speak more eloquently than ten thousand tongues. They are the messengers of overwhelming grief, of deep contrition, and of unspeakable love.

WASHINGTON IRVING

99

Feel Your Feelings

It's okay to feel your feelings. You don't have to repress your grief or sorrow or anger in order to be strong. Doing that doesn't magically make those feelings go away. No, instead those feelings fester inside of you, becoming darker and more intense, and they begin to eat away at you. Then they steal away your ability to find peace, heal yourself, forgive, and love.

When you give yourself the space and time to allow yourself to process how you are feeling, you will find that there is so much power in owning and understanding your emotions. Deeply felt emotion is what moves the world. Without grief, we would miss out on so much art and music created from loss. Jealousy, anger, and ambition all spur innovation and growth. Love and passion inspire us to make things better for everyone.

If you are strong enough to welcome your emotions, you are strong enough to use them to change the world.

100

We Affect Others

Talk not of wasted affection, affection never was wasted;
If it enrich not the heart of another, its waters, returning
Back to their springs, like the rain, shall fill them
full of refreshment.

HENRY WADSWORTH LONGFELLOW

We are all connected. As technology has advanced, we've all seen that for ourselves. A message shared in Ohio can end up inspiring someone in Hong Kong. Conservation efforts in Australia can help the fish near Hawaii. Drought-resistant crops developed in England can save children starving in Uganda.

What we do affects not just the people in our communities, but, people all over the world. War affects every economy. Drought and famine change migration patterns and send refugees searching for new homes. Disease can be spread as easily as breathing and travel as fast as an international flight.

But that is also true of peace. If we choose to work together to spread peace, understanding, kindness and love, what effect could that have?

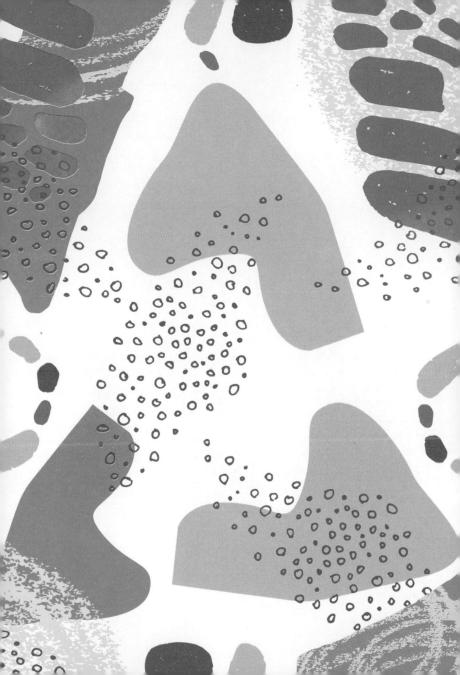

Notes

1. Aaron Hosman, "Newlyweds, Both Doctors, Spend Honeymoon Fighting Coronavirus," KCRG, April 4, 2020, https://www.kcrg.com/content/news/Cedar-Rapids-doctor--569383181.html.

2. "Fred Jordan Mission's 'Mother's Make-Overs' Kicks Off Week-Long Celebration for L.A.'s Impoverished Moms," Fred Jordan Mission, May 3, 2010, https://www.prnewswire.com/news-releases/fred-jordan-missions-mothers-make-overs-kicks-off-week-long-celebration-for-las-impoverished-moms-92674349.html.

3. "Bus Driver Who Caught Plunging Brooklyn Child Brushes Off 'Hero' Talk," *CNN*, July 18, 2012, https://www.cnn.com/2012/07/17/us/new-york-bus-driver-hero/index.html.

4. "How One Kidney Donation Kept On Giving," *CBS News*, August 6, 2008, https://www.cbsnews.com/news/how-one-kidney-donation-kept-on-giving/.

5. Dr. Ali Binazir, "Are You a Miracle? On the Probability of Your Being Born," *Huffpost*, August 16, 2011, https://www.huffpost.com/entry/probability-being-born_b_877853?guccounter=1&guce_referrer=aHR0cHM6Ly93d3cuZ29vZ2xlLmNvbS8&guce_referrer_sig=AQAAAJI3hmTJzvFQjWLh46PLZKV95xgCmeePGnWVeiooW6RtzgP0YAjrBBkcY-K1QZutn_9d2h4RwShvEy5OZxsVKUzPl-LP9f56oGr9CJYqeF333j_GpBnczAqpUYxuVZq3R3mckqkhAoDSCyVlq0rpbyewJM3lA4Xvqido Jgoud_jY.

6. Candace Buckner, "When the Virus Shut Down an English City, This Hotel Turned Itself into a Homeless Shelter," *The Washington Post*, June 23, 2020, https://www.washingtonpost.com/nation/2020/06/23/when-virus-shut-down-an-english-city-this-hotel-turned-itself-into-homeless-shelter/.

7. "Capt Sir Tom Moore Knighted in 'Unique' Ceremony," *BBC News*, July 17, 2020, https://www.bbc.com/news/uk-england-beds-bucks-herts-53442746.

8. Skylar Mitchell, "This Mom Donated Her Lottery Winnings to a Wounded Police Officer. Now the Community Is Paying Her Back," *CNN*, July 22, 2020, https://www.cnn.com/2020/07/22/us/mom-lottery-win-donation -trnd/index.html.

9. McKinley Corbley, "After Australian Bushfires, People Knit Mittens for Burnt Koalas and Raise Almost $2 Million to Help," Good News Network, November 29, 2019, https://www.goodnewsnetwork.org/people-knit -mittens-for-burnt-koalas-and-raise-money/.

10. "From Pizza to Fresh Vegetables: When You're in the Bronx, You're Going to Get Fed by This Generous Community," Good News Network, July 26, 2020, https://www.goodnewsnetwork.org/from-pizza-to-fresh-veggies -people-in-the-bronx-will-feed-you/.

11. Nicole Pelletiere, "Single Dad Adopts 13-Year-Old Who Was Abandoned 2 Years Earlier at Hospital," *Good Morning America*, March 2, 2020, https://www.goodmorningamerica.com/family/story/single-dad-adopts -13-year-abandoned-years-earlier-69285077.

12. Cathy Free, "She Was Furloughed from Her Job. So She Became 'Lasagna Lady' and Made 1,200 Pans of Free Lasagna for Those in Need," *The Washington Post*, June 24, 2020, https://www.washingtonpost.com /lifestyle/2020/06/24/she-was-furloughed-her-job-so-she-became -lasagna-lady-gave-away-1200-pans-free-lasagna/.

13. "Garbage Men Break Down in Tears When Residents Surprise Them with 'Thank You' Party Attended by Mayor," Backyard Bend, July 27, 2020, https://backyardbend.com/garbage-men-break-down-in-tears-when -residents-surprise-them-with-thank-you-party-attended-by-mayor/.

14. McKinley Corbley, "Boy Invites His Entire Kindergarten Class to His Adoption Hearing—and the Ceremony Was Incredibly Sweet," Good News Network, December 6, 2019, https://www.goodnewsnetwork.org /boy-invites-kindergarten-class-to-adoption-hearing/.

15. Jennifer Smith, "7 Benefits of Smiling and Laughing That You Didn't Know About," *Lifehack*, https://www.lifehack.org/articles/communication /7-benefits-smiling-and-laughing.html.

16. Casey Watts and Elena Cawley, "No Words Needed School's 'Happy Birthday' Video Goes Viral," *The Tullahoma News*, October 31, 2018, https://www.tullahomanews.com/news/local/no-words-needed-school -s-happy-birthday-video-goes-viral/article_99c9de2e-dc78-11e8-aae4 -9f9c756cbcbd.html.

17. Be My Eyes, Hans Jørgen Wiberg, https://www.bemyeyes.com/about.

18. Sara Gilgore, "How a Sterling Animal Care Biz Owner Landed on Animal Planet," *Washington Business Journal*, June 19, 2018, https://www.biz journals.com/washington/news/2018/06/19/how-a-sterling-animal-care -biz-owner-landed-on.html.

19. Jen Reeder, "'Cuddle Club' Unites Senior People and Senior Dogs in the Sweetest Way," *TODAY*, July 5, 2019, https://www.today.com/pets/cuddle -club-unites-senior-people-senior-dogs-muttville-rescue-t157777.

20. "SWAT Team Superheroes Drop by Colo. Children's Hospital," *Modern Healthcare*, September 22, 2018, https://www.modernhealthcare.com /article/20180922/NEWS/180929979/swat-team-superheroes-drop-by -colo-children-s-hospital.